Love, Life & Loss

Anthony Fye II

DEDICATION

First and foremost, I give honor to God, from whom all blessings flow. None of this would be possible without Him. Thank You for the gift of creativity, for allowing me to express myself, and for providing an outlet to navigate the many emotions, thoughts, and feelings I wrestle with daily.

To my muses, both known and unknown, thank you for inspiring me. Your presence, your lessons, and even your absences have shaped me in ways I never expected. Some lessons came gently, like a whisper in the wind, while others arrived like storms, forcing me to grow in ways I never imagined. I am grateful for them all.

To my friends, family, and supporters, thank you. Many of you know that writing began as my therapy, a way to process complex thoughts and emotions. I never intended to share my words, let alone publish them for the world to read. Yet here I am, and that is in no small part because of your encouragement, your love, and your unwavering belief in me.

Thank you all for walking this journey with me. May God bless and keep you always.

CONTENTS

Introduction

In every life, there are moments when time seems to stand still, when love touches us so deeply that it changes the very fabric of who we are, and when loss leaves us searching for something to hold onto. This collection, Love, Life, and Loss, explores the complex journey through these emotions, weaving the delicate threads of joy, sorrow, and everything in between.

This collection moves through the seasons of love, its beginnings, its endurance, and its eventual fading. Alongside love, we explore the inevitable reality of loss, not as a finality but as an ongoing process of transformation.

Each poem within these pages is a snapshot of emotion, a brief moment in time where words attempt to capture the nuances of what it means to be human. Whether it's the quiet ache of love lost or the bittersweet remembrance of a life once lived. Love, Life, and Loss invites the reader into a deeply personal space, one where vulnerability and strength coexist.

This is not merely a collection of poems but a journey through heartache, healing, and the resilience that comes with each new day. It is an invitation to reflect, to mourn, to celebrate, and ultimately, to embrace the beauty in the impermanence of life.

THE WORLD WAS ONCE A CANVAS

Painted in colors only a child could see.

As we grew and time went, those vibrant hues
Somehow seemed to fade,
Our hearts on fire and eyes once opened wide,
Grew cold and closed as life taught lessons
We never wanted to learn.

Dreams once bloomed like spring's first flower,
Soft petals untouched by bitter frost.
But seasons changed, and so did we,
Chasing shadows, losing light,
Trading wonder for the weight of knowing.
We wore masks not made for play,
But to shield the truth we couldn't say.

In youth, the moon was a beacon of mystery,
Whispering secrets to the stars.
But now, it looms a pale reminder
Of things we longed for and never found.

Anthony Fye II

The sun once kissed our cheeks in gold,
Now it burns, unyielding, harsh,
Its brilliance a glare we squint against.

Voices once sang with laughter's melody,
Each note a promise of endless days.
But they grew faint, and silence crept in,
Echoing with questions left unanswered.
We held hands, tight and trusting,
But fingers slipped, and distances grew.
What once united now divides,
Love wrapped in fear, truth hidden in lies.

Do you remember the endless skies,
The clouds we swore were castles?
Now they dissolve into shapeless gray,
No magic left in their fleeting forms.
The rain that danced in rhythm with our joy
Falls heavier now, soaking through,
A reminder that nothing stays dry forever.

We walked barefoot through fields of innocence,
Each step is a soft imprint on unbroken soil.

Now the ground is rough, the grass worn thin,

Our paths tangled, leading nowhere clear.

We built dreams from sand, towers reaching high,

But the tide came in, as tides always do,

And left us staring at the empty shore.

There was a time we feared the dark,

Huddling close to escape its grip.

Now we find comfort in shadows' embrace,

Hiding from truths too bright to face.

The monsters beneath our beds have gone,

But new ones linger in mirrors, in minds,

Their whispers louder than we'd like to admit.

Still, there's a flicker a faint, fragile light,

A shard of the child who painted the skies.

It calls through the haze, a quiet plea:

"Remember the colors. Remember the dream."

Though time may dull, it cannot erase

The moments when the world was new.

We carry them, etched in the soul's deepest place,

A secret reservoir of hope and hue.

Anthony Fye II

So as we wander, weary and worn,
Let us not forget where we've been.
For in the ashes of innocence lost,
Lie seeds of wisdom, waiting to bloom.
And though the world is no longer a canvas
Painted in colors only a child could see,
Perhaps we can learn to hold the brush,
And create new hues with what remains.

If Only I Had More Time

If only I had more time,
I'd tell you just how much you meant.
I'd tell you how I loved each day we spent,
How I cherished every sunrise, every sunset.

I'd remind you of the games we played,
The laughter shared, the moments in between,
The small things that meant the world to me,
Though to you, they may have seemed unseen.

Each tiny moment built a mountain of memories,
A fortress I lean on when I'm feeling low.
I'd tell you how much you taught me,
And how your strength gave me room to grow.

You set an example I'll always try to meet,
A guiding light when the path was unclear.
I'd thank you endlessly for the things you did,
The unseen efforts, the love so sincere.

Anthony Fye II

I'd tell you that you're never alone,
That your battles were my battles too.
Together, we could have faced any storm,
Together, we could have made it through.

If only I had more time,
I'd tell you how deeply I loved you,
How much you meant to me,
And the words I never had the chance to speak.

If only I had more time,
I'd say all the things left unsaid,
If only I had more time,
To hold you close and ease the regrets in my head.

What Will You Remember?

When I'm gone, what will you say of me?

Will you say I truly loved you,

And that I knew you loved me too?

Will you smile and whisper, "I'm glad you were here,

And I'm grateful I got to share my days with you."

Will you say, "I miss you,"

And wish we had just a little more time?

Will you recall the life we lived,

The laughter, the tears, the moments that made us whole,

The nights we dreamed together, heart and soul?

When I'm no longer here, what will you do?

Will you carry on with our favorite pastimes,

And find joy in the things we used to love?

Will you hear my voice in a favorite song,

Or see my face in the stars above?

When I leave, what will you remember?

Will you think of lazy days spent lounging,

Anthony Fye II

The quiet comfort of a shared silence,
Or the way I held your hand when words were few,
Letting you know I was there, just for you?

Will you remember my laughter,
The way it filled a room with light?
Will you think of my smile,
Or the times I held you close at night?

When I'm gone, I hope you find the strength
To cherish the memories we made,
To keep my love alive in your heart,
Even as the years begin to fade.

So when you think of me,
I hope it brings you peace,
I hope you find comfort in the love we shared,
And know that it will never cease.

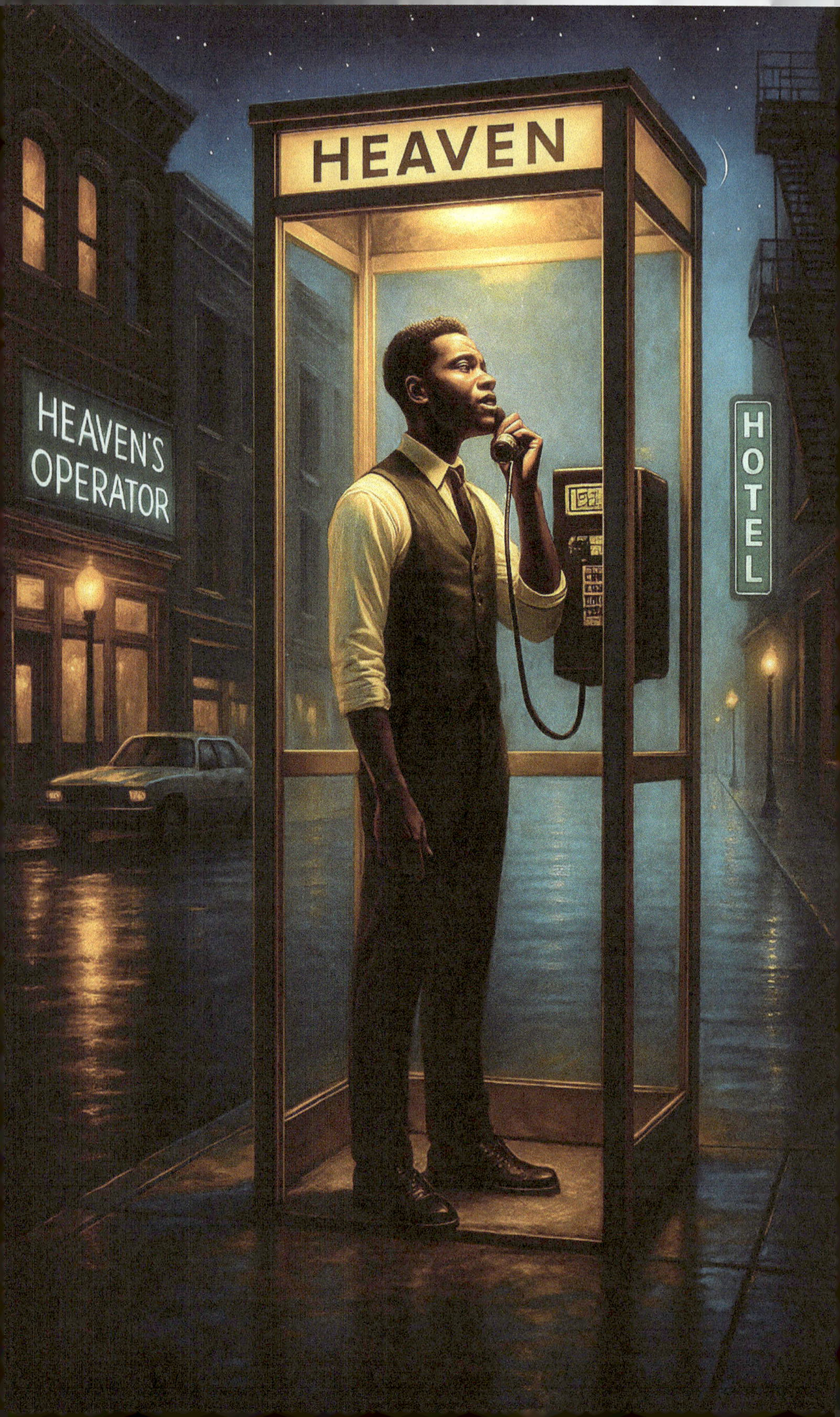
HEAVEN
HEAVEN'S OPERATOR
HOTEL

HEAVEN'S OPERATOR

Hey operator, yeah, it's me.

There's a couple of people up there I'd really like to see.

But since I can't hug them, I'll settle for speaking.

Can you get them all together?

Put me on speaker; I've got some things worth repeating.

And while you're at it, could you ask the Lord to come through?

I've got a few questions, and I really need the truth.

Hey everyone, I'm so glad you're all there.

You'll never know how much I miss you,

Or how deeply I wish that you were here.

I just wanted to update you on what's been going on.

I know you've been watching,

But watching's not the same.

Life's been moving fast, but I'm holding my ground.

I carry you with me; your love's all around.

Anthony Fye II

The holidays are harder; your laughter feels gone,
But your spirit reminds me to keep pressing on.

To the Lord, I must ask how do You heal a broken heart?
How do You hold us together when life falls apart?
Do they hear my whispers when I speak late at night?
Do they know I still love them? Are they safe in Your light?

To my loved ones, I hope you're proud of me now.
I'm walking the path we once mapped out somehow.
Your words still guide me, your lessons still teach.
Even in silence, you're never out of reach.

Operator, thank you for this moment in time.
A fleeting connection, yet it feels so divine.

One last thing before the line goes dead
I carry your love and the words you once said.
Until we meet again, I'll keep pushing through.
I promise to live a life worthy of you.

If there's a way to call again,
I'll be back tomorrow to talk to my friends.

THE PIECES YOU LEFT BEHIND

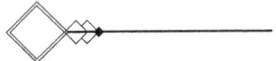

I find pieces of you in the things you left behind,

A shirt you used to wear,

That still smells like you,

No matter how many times I wash it your scent still comes through,

And with it come the memories of days spent well,

Making me wish I could hug you once more.

A game we used to play,

Your laughter still echoes in my mind.

Now it feels hollow, incomplete

It's not as much fun without you here.

A book you shared with me,

Its story incomplete.

How desperately I wish we could speak;

I'm scared to read the final page

Afraid of where it might leave me.

Anthony Fye II

A place we used to go,

Now silent and bare.

I sit alone, aching for the moments we can no longer share.

The old fishing spot we both loved,

Where the water carried your joy like the breeze.

Now it feels quiet, too still,

Missing the sound of your voice.

I find pieces of you in the things you left behind,

Your kindness, your courage, your light.

But of all the things you left behind,

I find the most of you in me.

DENIAL   ANGER   BARGINING   BARRANING   ACRES

THE CYCLE OF GOODBYE

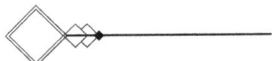

The hardest part of goodbye was not knowing it was our last.

I'm here without you now,

And it all happened so fast.

I thought I'd never be alone again,

But fate had different plans.

You left and you took a part of me,

Forever changing my reality.

I don't recognize this life or the world around me,

Looking at life through glasses without the right lenses

Shadows blending,

Mixing love and grief,

Terrible recipes, making me without you

Too bitter to chew.

I was meant to stand with you,

Not above you.

How dare you!!

How could you just leave me?

Anger rises like a storm,

As I scream into the silence,

But my voice fades to whispers,

And anger collapses into despair.

I bargain with memories,

Wishing for one more moment,

One more chance to turn back time.

Denial wraps itself around me,

A fragile shield to keep the pain at bay,

But cracks appear,

And reality seeps through in shades of gray.

This can't be real,

I tell myself, over and over.

This isn't my life.

And yet again, I try to bargain.

I make silent deals with fate

If only I could turn back time,

If only I could have one more moment.

But time doesn't listen,

It moves forward, dragging me with it.

Then sadness arrives,

Heavy as a rain soaked sky.

I retreat into its gray embrace,

Lost in the weight of what's been taken.

I retreat,

Lost in the weight of it all

Stuck in this pit of sadness and sorrows where time moves slow.

Every smile feels foreign,

Every breath feels heavy.

I wonder, will this ache ever go?

Just as I begin to feel numb,

Denial returns, like a whisper.

Maybe this is all a dream,

And I'll wake to find you here.

My mind clings to shadows of hope,

Even as reality presses in.

A cycle, relentless and raw.

I move between anger and sadness,

Anthony Fye II

Between bargaining and disbelief,
Until acceptance briefly flickers.

As days turn to weeks,
A faint light begins to shine.
Acceptance doesn't come in waves,
But in moments, small and kind.

I begin to feel you in the wind,
Hear you in the quiet of the stars.
Your absence doesn't mean you're gone
You're etched in my heart,
In every beat, every breath.

Acceptance doesn't end the pain
It just teaches me to carry it,
To hold it close,
To wear it like armor and not a chain.

But even then, the cycle begins again,
Grief spinning me in its orbit.
Love and loss intertwined,
An eternal loop of what was and what will always be.

The hardest part of goodbye

Was not knowing it was our last.

But the love you left behind

Still holds me fast.

THE ENDLESS DREAM

In quiet hours, when shadows drape the sky,
I whisper to the void, seeking you once more,
Your memory, a whisper, never says goodbye,
A presence felt, a bond still to the core.

Do you wander, dear, in fields of golden light,
Where time is but a ripple, endless, free?
Do you remember, dear, our talks in darkest night,
Or have you found a peace that's lost to me?

Your laughter lingers, like a distant song,
A melody that dances through my mind,
In realms where we belong, where we are strong,
In dreams that never end, our souls entwined.

I reach for you, through veils of sleep and tears,
Through echoes of a life that once was whole,
I search the endless dream where love adheres,
And find you there, a balm to my lost soul.

Anthony Fye II

Oh, to touch your face, to feel your warmth again,

To breathe the air where once we stood as one,

In dreams unbroken, love shall still remain,

An endless dream beneath the endless sun.

In waking hours, the world may seem so bleak,

Yet in the dream, your light forever gleams,

A solace for the heart, the soul's own peak,

In endless love, within the endless dreams.

This must be a dream

But I can't seem to wake.

THE DAY THE LIGHT CHANGED

I swear the sun was softer once,

Before I knew the weight of shadows.

I swear the sun I remember embraced us as children,

Wrapping us in warmth as we ran through open fields,

Laughing, chasing dreams too big for our hands to hold.

We wished for clear skies,

For dark clouds to drift far away,

Never knowing that one day,

We would crave the rain.

The shadows of the past were gentler

They held no secrets,

No fears,

No words left unsaid,

No grief that lingered like an echo in the soul.

But now, the rain falls heavier somehow,

Carrying the weight of hidden tears,

Falling in a storm so loud

It drowns the silence we once found comfort in.

And in that silence, we remember

We remember the days when life was simple,

When our laughter rose higher than the treetops,

When our innocence shielded us from the world's sharp edges.

We remember scraped knees that healed overnight,

Broken toys that could be fixed,

And the certainty that love was forever.

But somewhere along the way, we learned to fear.

We fear what we've lost,

Fear what we've done,

Fear what we've become.

We fear the mirror,

Because the eyes staring back

Are no longer the ones we once knew.

Somewhere along the way, we learned to hate.

We hate the weight we carry inside,

The bitterness that poisons,

The anger that consumes,

The way it shapes us into something unrecognizable.

We hate the questions that haunt us,

The regrets that refuse to be silenced.

We hate how we reach for the past,

Only to find it slipping through our fingers like sand.

And still, we chase.

We chase the warmth we once felt,

The trust we once had,

The belief that life would always be kind.

We chase the innocence we lost,

Knowing deep down we can never have it back.

And all the while, we wonder

When was the day the light changed?

Did the world shift, twisting us with it?

Or were we the ones who changed,

While the light remained the same,

Shining as it always has,

Though we can no longer feel it?

Anthony Fye II

Maybe the light never left.

Maybe it was us who learned to close our eyes.

Maybe we let the weight of pain eclipse the sun,

Mistaking our own darkness for the end of the light.

And maybe, just maybe,

If we stop running,

Stop counting what we lost,

Stop fearing what we've become,

We will feel the warmth again.

Maybe the sun is still soft.

Maybe the light was never lost.

Maybe we just forgot how to see it.

WHEN LOVE DIES

When love dies, it doesn't scream or shout,
It fades away, like a candle blown out.
The warmth once felt, now is just a chill,
A void that time alone can't fill.

The laughter shared turns into sighs,
Sweet words exchanged become goodbyes.
The sparkle fades from once-bright eyes,
And truth emerges from well spun lies.

You start to feel the growing space,
A chasm wide you can't embrace.
The hand you held now feels so cold,
The bond once new has grown so old.

Silent meals and empty stares,
The room is filled with unmet glares.
The spark that set our hearts ablaze
Has drowned beneath love's shifting haze.

Anthony Fye II

Promises made begin to crack,
Dreams we built fade to black.
We're strangers now, where lovers stood,
And love's sweet bloom has turned to wood.

No more talks of future plans,
No more fingers intertwined hands.
The "us" we built slips through our grasp,
The final breath of love's last gasp.

When love dies, it's not a flame,
But ashes left without a name.
It whispers out its last goodbye,
And leaves us with the question: Why?

But as it ends, we must let go,
To find a way to heal, to grow.
For when one love dies, another may bloom,
And light the shadows of this room.

EMPTY VOWS

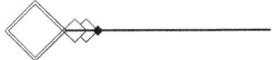

I could have treated you better, it's true,

But deep down, I wondered did you deserve it too?

I'm far from perfect; I've made my share of mistakes,

But respect is a choice that we both failed to make.

I gave you everything I had

My heart, my trust, my dreams so grand.

But you took them for granted, tossed them all aside,

Leaving me empty, with nowhere to hide.

I weathered the storms, endured the pain,

Held on tight through sunshine and rain.

Every sacrifice, every tear I shed,

Met with silence, words left unsaid.

I could have treated you better, yes,

If only you had seen me, felt the mess.

I bent, I broke, trying to make it right,

But you were gone, long before the fight.

Anthony Fye II

Now I stand, stronger somehow,
No longer tied to empty vows.
I'll heal, I'll learn, I'll find my peace,
From the love that failed, I'll find my release.

I deserved better; I see it now
A love that stands firm, not one that bows.
So here's to the future, a new chance to start,
With someone who'll cherish all of my heart.

THE CYCLE OF US

On
I love you,
You're my best friend,
Together, we're unstoppable,
We'll make it until the very end.

Off
This isn't working,
I needed more from you,
The silence between us,
The things left unsaid, too.

On again
I know you're sorry,
I'm sorry too,
We can try again,
Start fresh, and make it through.

Off again
We tried,

Anthony Fye II

We failed,
Maybe it's not meant to be,
Each step forward, two steps away,
Wandering in circles, lost in what we see.

On again
Reintroduced by a friend,
Hope you've been well,
Your message felt like fate,
I'm glad you decided to reach out,
A chance for us to rekindle, to start again
Or so I thought, until doubts returned again.

Off again
I don't know what I was thinking,
What made me believe things would change,
The same patterns repeating,
The same hurts we can't arrange.

On again
We've both grown up,
Lessons learned, wisdom earned,

Let's try this one last time,

Dreams once bright, now intertwined.

Off

Betrayed,

Broken,

A love that's been tested,

Now shattered, unspoken.

The cycle never ends,

Only the weight of regret remains,

Torn between hope and heartache,

And a love that never fully sustains.

Because love wasn't enough

And the lies were too many.

THE GHOST OF YOU

Do I miss you?

Hell nah.

But maybe the you you used to be,

The you who loved me and only me.

The you whose words weren't poison-tipped lies,

Whose hands weren't strangers,

Whose touch didn't bite,

The you who didn't carry betrayal in your back pocket

Like a secret weapon, waiting to strike.

Where's the you who stayed?

Who didn't make me wonder,

Who didn't leave me waiting

While you spent nights wandering

Wandering away from me,

From us,

From the promises you swore were unbreakable,

But shattered so easily,

Like my trust.

don't miss you.

I miss the illusion.

The ghost of who you pretended to be.

But that's all you were

A mirage in the desert of my hope,

And I'm done dying of thirst for something

That was never real.

Where's the you you used to be?

Hell, maybe you never were.

The mask has fallen, the truth laid bare,

You were only a shadow, never really there.

So, no I don't miss you, I miss the facade,

But I've found my strength, and I've made my peace with God.

I'm done chasing ghosts, done playing the fool

I've reclaimed my heart, and that's my golden rule.

BORN ALONE

Born alone,
to live alone.

Why is that so hard to understand?
We claw through existence,
chasing echoes of something more,
but the silence always follows,
stretching long and hollow
like a shadow with no light.

We give and we give,
as if sacrifice will change the verdict,
as if drowning in others
will somehow make us float.
But the weight never lifts
it only settles deeper,
pressing bone against soul.

We wander through life,
grasping for meaning,

for connection,

for proof that we are more than ghosts

haunting our own reflections.

Each attempt brings new hope,

a flicker of warmth in an otherwise cold world.

And yet, hope is the cruelest torment,

a whisper of something just out of reach,

dangling in the distance like a mirage

that vanishes when we step closer.

Each new hope brings new pain

the sting of emptiness,

the hollow ache of knowing

that nothing ever truly fills the void.

We stitch ourselves together

with fragile threads of expectation,

only to unravel at the seams.

But what are we really losing?

A dream? A delusion?

Or just another illusion

that we were ever anything but alone?

The world moves on, indifferent,
as we linger in doorways,
watching people fade into the distance,
replaying conversations in our heads,
searching for the moment they decided
we were too much or not enough.

We are ghosts before death,
fading in the periphery of crowded rooms,
lost in the spaces between words,
forgotten even as we stand in plain sight.
The mind turns inward,
a labyrinth of closed doors,
each one leading deeper into the dark,
each one whispering the same truth:

You were never meant to belong.

Born alone,
to live alone
but does that mean we must endure alone?

Anthony Fye II

Perhaps solitude is not a prison,

but a sentence,

one we carry without appeal,

without reprieve.

Perhaps we are not missing something,

but rather cursed with awareness,

trapped in the cruel knowledge

that connection is fleeting,

that people leave,

that even memories decay.

And so we wander,

not searching,

but surviving,

not hoping,

but enduring.

Born alone,

to live alone

and perhaps, in the end,

to vanish alone.

WHY DON'T THEY WANT ME?

Why don't they want me?
I ask the night, the wind, the silence.
Am I too much, spilling over,
Or too little, slipping through?

They reach for me with open hands,
Then pull away like a tide retreating.
Here, then gone
A presence, a shadow, an empty space.

I offer softness, I offer strength,
I give them light, I give them quiet.
Yet something in me
Or something missing
Leaves them searching elsewhere.

Is it my voice, too full of longing?
My heart, too eager, too bare?
Do they taste my soul
And find it lacking?

Anthony Fye II

I shape myself to fit their world,
Bending, folding, shrinking
But the more I change,
The less I feel like me.
And still, they leave.
No words, no reasons,
Just a door left swinging,
A silence I must fill on my own.

I walk through memories,
Tracing laughter, unspoken truths,
Trying to find the flaw
The moment I became forgettable.

I wonder if I ask too much.
Not for riches, not for promises,
Just for presence,
For someone who stays.

Is love supposed to be fleeting?
Is connection so fragile
That a single word, a single moment,
Can send it unraveling?

I reach out, but hands slip through mine,

Like water refusing to be held.

I pour, I pour, I pour

And still, they thirst elsewhere.

What do they see in me?

A brief distraction,

A moment of warmth,

A temporary home?

I have tried to be softer,

To take up less space,

To demand nothing,

To be easy, effortless,

Yet even my absence goes unnoticed.

And so I sit with the quiet,

The questions looping in my mind,

The ache of never quite being enough,

Or always being too much.

Maybe I love too fiercely,

Hold on too tightly,

Anthony Fye II

Hope too deeply
Or maybe, just maybe,
I have been giving my love
To the wrong hands.

Maybe some people come
Only to leave.
Maybe I am not a home
They were meant to stay in.

Maybe the lesson
Is not in what I lack,
But in learning who deserves
The love I give so freely.

I will no longer beg,
No longer bend,
No longer make myself less
To be held for a moment.

I will not shrink to fit
Into hands that tremble at my weight.

I will not make myself small
For hearts that cannot carry me.

One day, someone will stay,
Not because I ask,
Not because I change,
But because they see me
And know I am enough.

And until that day,
I will love myself in the silence.
I will hold my own heart steady.
I will remind myself, again and again,
That I was never the problem.

STOLEN MOMENTS

Fleeting moments we cling to,
Stolen glimpses in a world that moves too fast.
We hold on tight to fragile dreams,
To things we know can never last.
A love so rare, it hides in the past,
Whispered through shadows we cannot outlast.

Nights dissolve into days too soon,
The stars retreat, replaced by the moon.
The sun breaks through, ending our embrace,
Pulling us apart, erasing your trace.
We steal time like thieves in the night,
Grasping seconds before they're out of sight.

We wish for time to slow its stride,
To freeze the world, to let us hide.
Just a moment, a breath, to have our fill,
Before the ticking clock exerts its will.
For every second that slips away
Takes pieces of the love we crave each day.

Stolen joy, a borrowed peace,

These moments are ours, though their time is brief.

The silence between us roars so loud,

Drowning the whispers of the restless crowd.

In this quiet, we build our space,

A world where time loses its race.

In secret, we find what others can't see,

A sanctuary for just you and me.

These hidden moments become our home,

A refuge for two hearts that roam.

The world fades out; it doesn't exist,

In the embrace of a stolen kiss.

Fleeting, yet deep, this love we defend,

Each second cherished, though it must end.

We live for the hours we steal away,

For a love that burns brighter than day.

The shadows might stretch, the night may fall,

But in this moment, we have it all.

There's beauty in the fleeting and rare,

A fragile love beyond compare.

Though time conspires to pull us apart,

It cannot erase what lives in the heart.

The minutes slip through like grains of sand,

Yet still, we hold them in trembling hands.

Every touch, every whispered word,

Becomes a memory that cannot be blurred.

The world may rush, and time may bind,

But here, in this moment, we leave it behind.

Our love exists where rules don't apply,

In stolen seconds beneath the sky.

Though the future looms with shadow and doubt,

And the light of dawn will find us out,

We cherish the now, the here, the real,

The fleeting moments that time cannot steal.

For even if tomorrow takes it away,

This love will echo beyond today.

So let us cling to the fleeting and rare,

To the stolen minutes that we dare to share.

The world may spin, the clock may chime,

But this love, in its moment, defies all time.

INVISIBLE IN THE CROWD

In this room full of people,

Where nobody sees me.

Pleasantries exchanged,

Ultimately meaningless.

Surrounded but not supported,

Like echoes in an empty hall,

Words bounce off the walls,

Yet no one hears my call.

I smile and nod on cue,

Playing the part they expect,

But inside I'm fading slowly,

A soul they fail to detect.

Loneliness in a crowd,

A silence that screams,

A feeling of invisibility,

Lost in everyone's dreams.

Anthony Fye II

I crave a deeper touch,
A gaze that holds my truth,
For someone to look beyond the mask,
And see the scars beneath the proof.

In this sea of strangers,
I drift like a leaf on the breeze,
Hoping for a hand to reach out,
To lift me from my knees.

A front painted on,
Desperate to hide pain,
The pain of holding on so hard,
To memories like a chain.

Smiling through the struggle,
Masking every tear,
Wishing you'd see the cracks,
Or sense the growing fear.

A fear of never being truly heard,
Of my voice lost in the noise,

Drowning in the empty chatter,
While silence steals my poise.

If you really listened though,
Then you'd finally realize,
I've told you a thousand times
Through quiet sighs and weary eyes,
In the silence between my lies.

I hide behind this fragile smile,
Afraid to let it break,
Longing for a moment of release,
To feel seen for my own sake.

I speak in unspoken words,
In glances that beg for care,
Hoping someone will notice
The weight of the pain I bear.

I just want to be seen,
Not just as a shadow in light,
But as a soul longing for connection,
A heart seeking what's right.

Anthony Fye II

Yearning for someone to notice
The silent screams inside,
To look beyond the surface,
And see where I truly hide.

In this crowded room, I'm lost,
A ghost in plain view
Longing for the day when someone
Finally sees me too.

LET ME SHOW YOU

I could tell you who I am, but you wouldn't believe me,

Probably think I'm just teasing

Like my words are wrapped in fiction,

Telling stories lacking conviction.

But if you watch closely, you'll see the truth:

No mask, no façade, just the real me,

Unfolding naturally, free to be.

I don't need to convince you with stories or schemes,

Painting myself in shades of dreams.

Let my soul do the speaking, raw and true.

I'll show you my heart through all I do.

I can tell you who I am,

But I'd rather show you.

You see, talk is easy, and words come cheap,

But with my actions, I'll give you something concrete.

Watch me set this love in stone,

Make it something meant to last

To pass the test of time,

Unlike the last.

Let go of past times and live in this moment with me.

Let me show you who I am in the way I hold you,

Enfold you in an embrace so sweet,

As the scent of me gently mingles with the fragrance of you,

Creating something beautifully new.

Let me show you who I am in the things I do for you.

Watch as I make mountains move for you,

Soothing storms, turning skies from gray to blue.

Let me write our love in the clouds

A masterpiece in the heavens, pure and proud,

Etched in the stars, a silent vow.

Let me show you who I am in the quiet nights,

In whispered words under softened lights,

In steady hands that'll never let go,

And a heart that beats just to let you know

I Am yours.

Let me show you who I am in every small way,

In every look, every word I say.

No need for promises or grand designs

Just this steady love, yours and mine.

TEACH ME HOW YOU LOVE YOU

Teach me how to love you right,

I've tried my way, but lost the light.

Is love for you in hands entwined,

Or in the whispers of hearts aligned?

Is it found in soft, sweet flowers,

Or stolen, tender midnight hours?

Is it kisses pressed upon your brow,

A quiet promise, here and now?

Is it laughter shared when skies are grey,

Or words unspoken that pave the way?

Is it in the comfort of knowing I'm near,

To calm your storms and ease your fear?

Is love the spark that ignites our souls,

The steady flame that keeps us whole?

Or is it patience through life's demands,

A touch, a glance, that understands?

Anthony Fye II

Teach me the rhythm, show me the rhyme,
I'll learn your heart, give it my time.
For love is a language I'll strive to know,
If you guide me, I'll let it grow.

Let me be your anchor, your place of peace,
The warmth that helps your doubts release.
Show me the love that makes you stay,
And I'll give it to you every day.

THE TASTE OF A KISS

I'm not really a kisser,

But I can't help imagining your lips on mine.

Would they taste like honey,

Or something darker, more divine?

I can't help but wonder,

Would your kiss cast a spell?

If so, what would it do?

Would I see your portrait in the stars of the night sky,

Or would I fall in love so deep,

I'd be forever incomplete without you in my life?

Would the touch of your lips linger,

Or tease like a fleeting sigh?

Would your breath warm my skin,

As we melt into the night's cry?

Would your kiss cause your hands to wander,

Tracing paths unspoken, unseen?

Fingers brushing mine

Anthony Fye II

A spark igniting tingles down my spine.

I'm not really a kisser, but
The thought of us isn't just ephemeral;
It's fire given life by the look in your eyes
Soft and consuming.
Your lips, your eyes, your heat
They've woven a dream I can't escape.

I'm really not a kisser,
But for you, I'd break all my rules.
To taste your desire, to drown in your pull,
And surrender completely, unapologetically
To the sway of our rhythm, the power of us.

BRAVE ENOUGH FOR ONE MORE TRY

I hesitated at the edge,

Memories whispering warnings from before.

As I paused, I listened

To the murmurs in the wind,

The subtle voices of caution

Wrapped in layers of past hurt.

I remembered being broken

Pain too terrible to bear.

Fragments of my heart scattered,

Pieces of my spirit lost somewhere,

Left behind in the aftermath,

A map of sorrow traced upon my soul.

I remember bending low,

Picking up shards of dreams

With trembling hands,

Feeling my soul laid bare,

Exposed, vulnerable, raw,

Each fragment sharper than the last,

Anthony Fye II

Every edge cutting deeper,
Drawing blood and tears alike.

The memories show me clearly
All the ways I was led astray,
Every misstep, every illusion,
Every promise whispered softly
Only to become silence in time.
They show me shadows
In places I once trusted to hold the light.

These whispers warn me sternly
Guard your heart, shield your soul,
Hide your true self away,
For safety lies in solitude,
Where no other hands can reach you,
Where no voice can deceive you
With tender words that only fade.

Memory makes the fall feel inevitable,
Makes the breaking seem unavoidable,
As if the past were a prophecy,
Destined always to repeat,

Chains forged from disappointment,

Locked in place by doubts and fears,

Weighing down my hesitant feet.

But standing here, on the edge,

Something in me shifts.

Looking out, not just with eyes,

But with my heart, my spirit, I see

I glimpse a horizon filled with newness,

With hope lingering gently in the distance,

Soft as morning's first light,

Real and gentle as a whispered prayer.

I stand on the edge, yes,

But it is an edge of possibility.

I see new pathways stretching

Beyond old hurts, beyond the shadows

Of the pains I've known before.

I see fresh chances painted in colors

I had nearly forgotten existed

Vibrant, warm, tender hues

Of possibility and hope.

Yes, the potential for pain
And breaking remains,
Woven into the very fabric of love,
For to love is always to risk,
To offer one's heart openly
Without certainty, without assurance,
Except the certainty of bravery itself.

Yet I remind myself softly
I have broken before,
Shattered completely,
But each breaking taught me
How to mend, how to grow,
How to transform pain into wisdom,
How to rise and gather my strength
From the scattered pieces of yesterday.

So, standing here,
With the wind whispering caution,
I choose instead to listen
To the gentle voice within
The voice brave enough to hope again,

To trust again,

To love again.

I release my breath, step forward,

Reaching beyond doubt,

Stepping beyond fear,

Choosing courage over caution,

Trusting heartache won't define me

Only strengthen me, refine me.

Yet here I am, reaching out once more,

Unafraid of the uncertain sky,

Embracing hope, daring love

Brave enough,

Strong enough,

Worthy enough,

Simply enough

For one more try.

Anthony Fye II

The Love Within

I want to fall in love again,
This time, it starts with me,
Not with fleeting glances,
But in my own reflection, free.

It won't be the first try,
But this time, I'll get it right,
Not chasing shadows of approval,
But embracing my inner light.

I want the joy it brings,
Like the warmth of a summer breeze,
The calm of picnics in the spring,
And love as steady as the trees.

I'll chase new feelings and experiences,
Like sunrises I've never seen,
Exploring paths untraveled,
And dreams I've yet to dream.

I'll focus on myself,

Treating me with care,

Mending all the broken pieces,

With love only I can bear.

No longer seeking it in others,

But in the way I rise each day,

In how I learn to heal my heart,

And gently push the pain away.

I'll laugh at my own jokes,

Dance to my own beat,

Cherish every flaw,

And find my soul complete.

So here I stand, unbroken,

Learning to love who I see.

This time, the love I find

Will start and end with me.

LOVE WASN'T THE PROBLEM

I used to say I'd never do this again,

Falling in love made me weak.

It left me breathless, drowning,

Grasping for hands that were always out of reach,

Gasping for air that was never meant for me.

So I swore off love

Not because I didn't want it,

But because I never expected to be loved properly.

I thought love was something I gave away,

Not something that would ever find its way back to me.

I spent so long believing love was pain,

That to love meant to lose,

That affection was currency,

Spent and never returned.

I braced myself for the fall.

But then I met you,

And now I'm starting to think

Anthony Fye II

I may have spoken too soon.

Because being loved by you
And loving you in return
Doesn't feel like weakness.
It doesn't feel like sacrifice or suffering.
It feels like breathing again
After being underwater for too long.
Like fresh air filling the lungs of a drowning man,
So sweet, so necessary, so unexpected.

And I hope you understand,
As I do,
Or at least as I'm beginning to,
That love was never the problem
It was who I gave it to.

There's something about the way you look at me,
The way you listen,
The way you don't make me feel
Like I have to prove my worth.

It doesn't feel like losing myself to someone else,

Like running in circles for something just out of reach.

It feels different.

Like the first rays of sunlight after a long storm,

Warming skin that has only known the cold.

Like standing on the shore,

Feeling the tide kiss your feet,

The waves no longer pulling you under,

But carrying you forward, gently, patiently.

Like the stillness of a meadow at dawn,

Where the air hums with quiet possibility,

And every blade of grass trembles

With the promise of something new.

Like the scent of rain on dry earth,

A promise of renewal,

A whisper that even what was once parched and withered

Can be full of life again.

It feels like the quiet of snowfall in the deep of winter,

The kind that slows the world,

Anthony Fye II

Makes you pause, makes you wonder,
Makes you believe that even in the coldest seasons,
There is beauty worth waiting for.

And yes, this is new,
But all the same,
It makes me wonder.

Maybe, just maybe,
Love was never the enemy.
Maybe I was just waiting
For the right reason to believe again.

And maybe, just maybe,
That reason is you.

COUNT THE DAYS

I often sit back and count the days of my life.

I reflect and wonder how did I get to this point?

I count the days when I was down,

The moments when the weight of the world sat heavy on my chest.

I count the nights I spent in silence,

Staring at the ceiling, drowning in my own thoughts.

I count the scars some visible, some unseen,

Each one a story, a lesson, a wound that once refused to heal.

I count the times I broke apart,

The days I stood in front of the mirror,

Searching for the person I used to be.

I count the pieces of my heart,

Scattered like shattered glass,

Picking them up, turning them over in my hands,

Trying to make sense of what's left.

I count the memories I've lost,

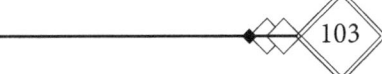

The laughter that faded into echoes,

The hands I once held but no longer reach for me.

I count the words left unsaid,

The apologies never given,

The love that slipped through my fingers like grains of sand.

I count the ways I felt unworthy,

The moments I believed I wasn't enough,

The times I turned away from love

Because I thought I didn't deserve it.

But then… I count something new.

I count my way back to the day I met you,

A moment so unexpected, yet it changed everything.

I count the first time your name felt like home,

The first time your voice quieted the noise in my mind.

I count the smiles you brought back to my face,

The warmth that filled spaces once left cold.

Now, I count the blessings each day since you arrived,

Each sunrise holding the promise of something more.

Now, knowing you, I see that not being the same is okay.

The cracks in me no longer feel like flaws,

But reminders of the light you helped shine through them.

I count the miles that keep us apart,

The distance that stretches between my longing and your embrace.

I count the nights I fall asleep reaching for you,

The mornings I wake up wishing you were here.

I count the letters of your name,

Tracing them in my mind like a prayer.

I count the days, the hours, the minutes until I can hold you again.

And then, I stop counting.

Because in you, I have found what I never thought I deserved.

Because love is not measured in numbers,

Not counted in distance, time, or past mistakes.

It simply is.

And in this revelation, I finally accept

I am worthy of love.

Anthony Fye II

I am worthy of you.
And for the first time, I no longer count the days I lost,
Only the ones I have left to love you.

STARDUST AND LAWN CHAIRS

Under a velvet quilt of night,
We sink into these old lawn chairs,
Side by side, we gaze at the stars
Two travelers in the quiet air.

How did we get here, love?
Not the first hands we held,
Not the first hearts that we adored,
But the ones that time compelled.

Your hair, now silvered with the moon,
Mine thin, a crown of fading years,
We speak in murmurs of old dreams,
Of winding paths and disappeared fears.

We weren't each other's first
But what sweet madness it is, to be last.
To find a home in this fleeting life,
Despite the bruises of the past.

Anthony Fye II

I wonder if the stars once guided us,
In those separate, distant skies.
Did they pull us like tides together,
Through all our hellos and goodbyes?

The laughter of long-lost loves
Still dances in the spaces between,
But here we are, the sum of all,
The remnants of what once had been.

We've lived lives full of other names,
Felt other kisses in the dark.
But now, here in this backyard,
We are each other's final spark.

The stars do they remember the nights
We lay with others and made our vows?
Or do they only see us now,
Holding on to our wrinkled brows?

In this tender, twilight moment,
I feel the years slip from our bones.

We may not be each other's first,

But we've made this love our home.

So we lie here, old and weathered,

Not wondering where we lost our youth.

For in your hand I've found forever,

And in your eyes, an endless truth.

Let the stars keep their secrets,

Of all the lives we've left behind.

Tonight we rest in the wonder

Of the love we chose to find.

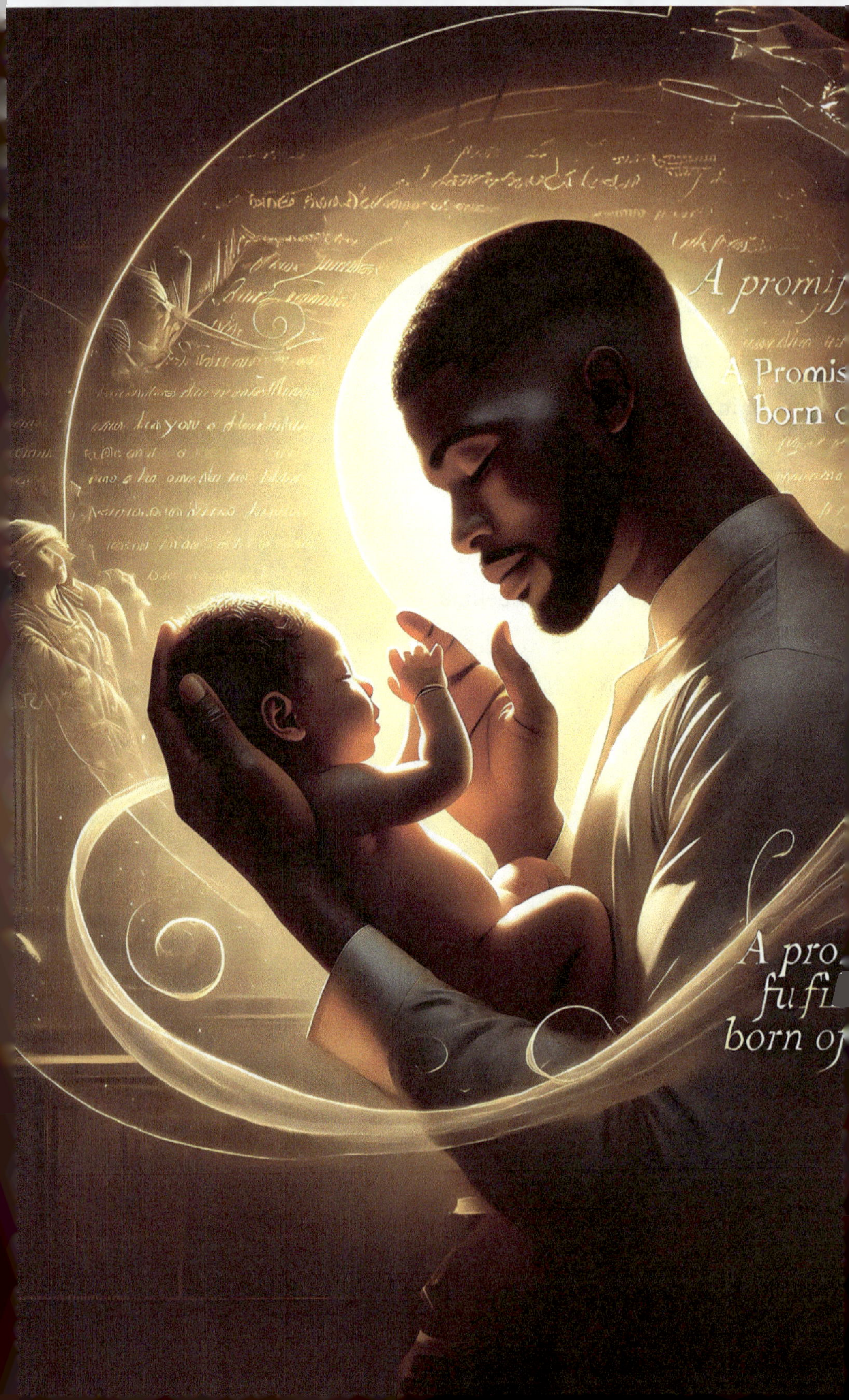

A Promise Fulfilled, Born of Love

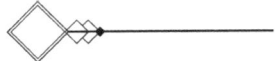

Born of love,

You changed my life.

Held in my hands,

Lost in a new world, as you became mine.

Love made manifest,

I held my hopes and dreams in my hands,

Dreaming of a future that only I could see

A future unspoken, yet grand, filled with possibility.

A heart expanded,

A depth of love I never knew,

A love that grows with each passing day

Endless, unyielding, in every way.

It stretches beyond what words can say,

A bond that will never fade or stray.

A dream come true

You may not know, but I always wanted you.

Long before I saw your face,

Anthony Fye II

I imagined your laugh, your smile, your grace.
I dreamed of the day
When I'd hold you close and watch you play.

A prayer answered.
Through every prayer, every whispered wish,
I silently hoped for this bliss
A dream of you, beyond what I could see,
A miracle unfolding, meant to be.

In quiet moments, I asked God
For a love like yours to light my life.
I prayed for the joy you'd bring to my days
For laughter, for lessons, for love that stays.

I longed for the moments we'd share,
For your heart, your spirit, your light to care.
The future, once uncertain, now so bright
With you, my son, the world feels right.
Through every prayer, through every plea,
I found you, my gift, my eternity.
A promise fulfilled in your every breath,
A love that transcends both life and death.

THE RUINS WE LEFT BEHIND

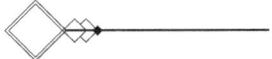

We built castles out of dreams,

Only to watch them crumble with time.

Time became the enemy in our minds,

A thief that stole the light from our eyes,

That whispered doubt into the spaces

Where hope once bloomed.

We watched the world shift,

Felt the ground give way beneath our feet,

Tried to speak against the wind,

But the echoes drowned us out.

We tried to breathe new life into old dreams,

To patch the fractures with whispered prayers,

But no matter how we held on,

No matter how tight our grip,

Dreams did fall,

Dreams did crumble.

And when the dust had settled,

We found ourselves among the ruins,

Anthony Fye II

Sifting through the jagged remnants
Of what once felt indestructible.
We cut ourselves on the sharp edges of memory,
Bled onto the stones of our past,
Yet still, we stayed.

We built temples in the wreckage,
Turned our sorrow into sacred shrines,
Kneeled before the altar of our old lives,
Bruised, bleeding,
Afraid to move,
Afraid to let go.

We wept in the halls of what once was,
Tangled in the chains of nostalgia,
Believing them to be unbreakable,
Until one day
We looked down and saw
That the chains were untethered,
That the walls were built from our own grief.

We had held ourselves captive,
Locked ourselves in a prison of the past,

While time, indifferent and unyielding,

Moved on without us.

And so, we moved too.

Not because the pain had faded,

Not because the wounds had healed,

But because we finally understood

We could not live in the ruins forever.

We stepped beyond the temple doors,

Into the light of a world we had abandoned.

The air was strange,

The sky unfamiliar,

Yet possibility pulsed beneath our feet.

Still, we bled.

Still, we ached in places

We did not have words for.

Still, we flinched when the past

Reached for us in the night.

But we moved.

Anthony Fye II

And in our wandering,

We met others along the way

Some who carried their own ruins,

Some who turned away from our pain,

Some who did not see us at all.

We bled on those who never cut us,

Wounded those who had done no harm,

Until we learned,

Until we understood.

Pain unhealed is pain transferred.

Suffering left unchecked will spill over,

Drowning the innocent and the undeserving.

Somewhere along the way,

The cuts began to close.

The bruises, once dark and aching,

Faded into something softer.

And the fear, once a shadow at our backs,

Became a lesson we carried,

Not a master we obeyed.

We still look back sometimes,

Still feel the echoes of all we lost.

But we no longer kneel at the altar of our suffering,

No longer build prisons out of grief,

Nor castles,

Nor temples.

We built castles out of dreams,

Only to watch them fall.

Now, with steady hands and open hearts,

We lay the stones of something lasting.

We carve new beginnings from the wreckage,

Not chasing towers, but building truth

And this time,

Time is not the enemy.

IF YOU LOVE ME

If you love me, tell me now

Don't wait until it's too late.

If you love me, say it now,

So I can say, "I love you too," before fate.

If you love me, show me now,

For I may not be here long.

If you love me, listen now,

I have words that need to belong.

If you love me, call me now,

I need the comfort of your voice.

If you love me, see me now,

While we still have the choice.

If you love me, acknowledge me

Let me know you see me clear.

If you love me, forgive me now,

I know I've stumbled through the years.

Anthony Fye II

If you love me, appreciate me,
Show me that I matter to you.
If you love me, hold me close,
While we still have moments, precious and few.

Don't wait for tomorrow,
For tomorrow may not come.
If you love me, let me feel it now,
While our hearts beat as one.

VILLAIN IN YOUR STORY

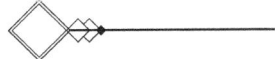

I'll be the villain in your story,
If that's what helps you sleep.
I'll wear the cloak you've cast on me,
But my soul, you cannot keep.

You paint me with the darkest brush,
A figure of your pain.
But shadows cannot hide the truth;
The light still calls my name.

If casting blame brings you peace,
Then blame me as you will.
But my steps are guided by a path
Much higher than your hill.

I won't trade my purpose for your anger,
Or my calling for your shame.
I know the One who gives me strength,
And He knows my true name.

Anthony Fye II

Call me selfish, call me cruel,
Say I failed you when you fell.
But I won't let your version of me
Rewrite what I know well.

I am not your scapegoat, though
I'll carry that weight with grace.
For forgiveness blooms in my own heart,
Even if yours leaves no trace.

You see a villain in my actions,
But God sees my intent.
While you spin tales of my destruction,
I seek His covenant.

Each stone you throw becomes a step
That lifts me closer to His throne.
And though you may not understand,
I know I'm never alone.

Your judgment may sting, but it cannot bind,
For freedom flows in truth.

And truth is this: I'm chosen still,
Redeemed in Spirit's youth.

Say what you must, tell all your tales
I won't demand you stop.
For I know that truth stands tall and strong,
While falsehoods always drop.

Your arrows fall before they pierce;
Your weapons hold no sting.
 For I am shielded by His grace,
And covered by His wings.

Let me be your shadowed figure,
The one you love to blame.
But know this heart beats steadily
With an everlasting flame.

A flame that burns for higher things
For love, for peace, for grace.
And even when you see me dark,
I'll strive to shine my face.

Anthony Fye II

Your anger's roar cannot consume me,
Your lies cannot define.
For truth is stronger than your hate,
And God's love makes it shine.

So go ahead, rewrite the script;
Make me the cause of your despair.
But know I kneel before the One
Who wipes my burdens bare.

It's not my job to change your heart,
Or heal the wounds you keep.
I'll leave that work to God above,
And pray for you in sleep.
For though you call me enemy,
I hold you in my prayer
That one day you'll release the weight
Of anger you can't bear.

Until that day, I'll carry on,
Obedient to His call.
For the One who knows my every step
Will catch me if I fall.

I'll be the villain in your story,

If that's what sets you free.

But it won't stop me from walking

The path that God has laid for me.